ypny
your planet needs you

"I would be very surprised if this beautifully designed handbook didn't inform you, provoke you, and motivate you to do your bit for a better world."

Sir Jonathon Porritt
Founder Director, Forum for the Future, Chair UK Sustainable Development Commission.

"Mother Earth calls us to action from every page of this beautifully crafted book; please hear her call."

Nick Hart-Williams
Filmmaker, Director of Be the Change conference.

" There are big books, scary books, denial books and boring books about the human predicament. This one is so quick and easy to read, so well illustrated and covers the whole system so well there can be no sound reason for not reading it and passing it on to all your friends from children to the aged. "Your Planet needs You" is challenging, but not depressing and it gives us all something to do about it."

Sir John Whitmore
Author, business consultant and organiser of Be the Change conference.

Jon Symes has produced a book that truly gets it right. Each page is a gem in itself, and taken together, they lead you to the conclusion that not only does your planet need you, but you definitely need your planet.
In clear, concise language and evocative images, we learn the true dire state of the world, why we have unintentionally caused this state and what we can do to turn the situation around.
This book is one of the elements of a world-wide emergence of a just, sustainable and spiritually fulfilling world.
Buy this book for everyone you know!

Jonathan Love
Director of the Awakening the Dreamer initiative of the Pachamama Alliance.

This book is dedicated to the element in all of us
that hears the call to play a part in creating a peaceful,
just and sustainable world.

ypny

your planet needs you

The water photographs have been reproduced by kind
permission of I.H.M.Co., Ltd.
with authorisation number ihm 0604120582
Images and Illustrations have been reproduced by kind
permission of the creators
A CIP catalogue record for this book is available from the
British Library

Published by Your Planet Needs You
13 Eaton Avenue
Chester, Cheshire
CH4 7HB
United Kingdom, 2006

ISBN 0-9553071-0-4
ISBN (new format) 978-0-9553071-0-2

Printed on 100% Recycled Paper (PEFC Certified)
Printed and bound by: Druckerei Uhl GmbH & Co KG,
Rober -Gerwig - Str. 35, 78315 Radolfzell, Germany

Graphic Design, Typography and Art Direction by Phil Turner
TURNER GRAPHIC DESIGN
www.philturner-uk.com

Contents

Acknowledgments

This book is dedicated to the element in all of us that hears the call to play a part in creating a peaceful, just and sustainable world.

Jon: my gratitude extends to all who have helped in the creation of this book, whether directly and knowingly or simply as the teachers who I have encountered in so many guises throughout my life.

In particular I honour and thank:
• my parents, Keith and Brenda who helped to shape my values and gave me a love of learning, of books and a deeper sense of curiosity about this world
• my children, Jack and Becky; my love for them and my concern for the future well-being of their whole generation have been my inspiration
• Phil, the creative genius who has picked up, embellished and given form to my ideas and so ensured that the book embodies its intention as a mission of love
• my partner, Sandra, who continues to inspire my love for her and for this mission.

Phil: my thanks go out to Jon for giving me the opportunity to design his book, to communicate his words and to enjoy creating with words and pictures, the process has been a wonderful journey and those close to me have travelled that journey too, thankyou. My thanks also to Nick Diggory for getting the ball rolling and asking his fellow illustrators and creatives to get involved, along with all the other illustrators who answered the brief contributing their ideas and committing their time to make the book what you see today.

Jointly: this creation has only been possible with the encouragement, advice, input and feedback of a number of people, particularly Barbara Allan, Martin Dewhurst, Paula Madan, Robin Cowan, Tina Symes, Trisha Hills, Deirdre Stubbs, Graham and Lindsay Flower and Christopher Barrat; each of you have added a layer of insight to ours.

A host of illustrators, artists and creative souls have submitted illustrations for the book; we are indebted to them all for their generosity of spirit and creativity. Although we haven't been able to use all of the work here, we are showcasing as much as we can at the website, www.yourplanetneedsyou.org. All of the featured illustrators are listed in the back of the book.

Sincerely Thank You

Introduction

The world is calling forth the very highest response from this generation. The greatest talents and attributes of the human race are needed in this time of extraordinary crisis and threat.

Previously, humankind has shown ingenuity, determination and resolve whenever crisis has threatened; we need those same characteristics now. There is, however, an additional dimension of response required today because we can't solve the complex and interlinked issues that we face with the level of thinking that created them. A fix-it mentality won't solve the climate problem or the global inequality that haunts us any more than scraping ice off the windscreen changes the weather. This particular fix might help us see to drive the car but it won't do away with ice. Fixes can only defer the problem or offset the symptoms; they don't deliver fundamental change.

The problems we face are rooted in the way we live and the way we think, so these are what must change. A new, higher level of thinking will usher in a new way of living, in which social justice and environmental sustainability are enshrined and where there is no concept of exploiting other people or damaging our home, Planet Earth. We need every ounce of our ingenuity, determination and resolve right now to build this future.

This book shows a simple, inescapable truth, that we are all co-creators of this future. The aim of the book is to spread the understanding of this reality and help us to see that we each have the ability to respond positively to the world situation, that response-ability rests with us.

Chapter One is a picture of the world we want for ourselves and for future generations. We need this clearly in view to guide us toward its creation. The core elements are described but you are invited to thread your own vision into this; your own personal interpretation of this magnificent goal will serve as your inspiration and motivation.

The Second Chapter reveals how we as individuals are each intimately involved in causing the world that we live in, even unconsciously. We examine too the thought forms that have risen to dominate our current thinking.

In Chapter Three we take a snapshot of the world at the beginning of the 21st century in order to see the scale and range of the issues we face. This picture is the shocking counterpart to the alluring vision of the first chapter. Together, as carrot and stick, they form an imperative for our action.

The book pivots at **Chapter Four** with the revelation of the simple and inescapable truth of our response-ability and the dilemma that this presents each of us.

In Chapter Five we turn to the personal response, which is Action. There are five principles to help us decide how best to focus our energy to make a difference in the world.

Then in Chapter Six we turn inward to look at our own Awareness. Once again there are principles to provoke and extend our own thinking as we step ever more purposefully into the personal changes which our world situation is demanding of each of us. This is the journey within.

Chapter Seven pulls together the themes of the book and provides a space for you to summon up your own response to the great challenge of creating our future.

At the end of the book you will find a full list of the sources that we have drawn on in writing the book and resources you can use to investigate any of the topics in more detail. The globe symbol ● in the text corresponds with information in Sources and Resources.

This flow of ideas is designed to help evoke your response to the challenges we face and so we recommend that at first sitting you read it sequentially. It is also designed to serve as a repository of inspiration and is a book you can dip into whenever you want a fresh slant or different insight. The intention is to inspire people to take whatever Action they wish, without constraint, so we offer principles for you to creatively interpret rather than prescriptive lists. There are other excellent references already in print and online which complement our approach with considerable detail; several are recommended at the back of the book.

We have also chosen to focus on the personal response each of us might take to a complex world situation because we believe this is a vital, overlooked part of the solution. Our current power structures cannot raise

themselves to the new level of thinking required without our voice, as consumers, citizens and voters.

Nonetheless the work of reinventing these structures is a vital part of creating the future we want; we leave it to other authors to show how best to reform our economic, political and education systems to better serve the world we are creating. Business deserves a special mention. It is an easy target for criticism because of the huge injustice and damage done by corporations around the world. But business itself isn't intrinsically bad, it is perhaps just a vehicle helping individuals to play out their own wants and desires in the world, as employees and as consumers. The work of creating a new paradigm in which it becomes a powerful tool for improving the well being of humankind is also crucial: this too lies outside the scope of the book.

Our final thought about how to get the most from the book is to share it. Please pass it around to help spread the ideas and energy that flow from it.

Our motive for writing this book has been to find out how we can best offer our contribution to the most important work of our time, building ourselves a sustainable future. We suspect this is the same motivation that has caused you to pick it up. The process of writing has been incredibly rewarding. We have discovered first hand the truth that we can't make a difference in the world until we start the process of change within ourselves. We are both still in that process, so write from the road as fellow travellers and not from the destination as self-appointed experts. We hope the insight we are gaining from our own experience of Action and Awareness is inspiration for your journey, both within and without.

a future worth choosing

RESPECT FOR GAIA

LIVING VALUES

FAIR SHARES

EVER AFTER THINKING

Can we...

save the human race from itself ?

We've reached the moon, split the atom, probed outer space and the inner workings of our bodies; our achievements seem boundless, except the most important of all, **saving us from ourselves.**

We've occupied every corner of the globe and subjugated every other life form but we haven't yet mastered ourselves. The human race is running out of control, cannibalising its own home in an orgy of consumption. We know the situation is about to implode but we simply haven't been able to stop ourselves. And today the symptoms of this are getting ever closer to home; televised images of human suffering, inhuman cruelty and environmental devastation.

It would be easy to sink into resigned apathy, or perhaps to party on as if we haven't heard the news. Alternatively we can choose a different response, that of working for a better world, which is one we can enjoy today but designed to last beyond tomorrow. The very fact that you are reading this book shows that you have heard this call and recognise the opportunity to contribute your energy to this wonderful vision, building a Future Worth Choosing.

'Your Country Needs You' was the old rallying call of Uncle Sam and Lord Kitchener in times of national crisis, now we face a crisis for the whole human race, so the call goes out;
Your Planet Needs You

A Future Worth Choosing has four core elements:

1. **FAIR SHARES,** 2. **LIVING VALUES,**
3. **RESPECT FOR GAIA** 4. **EVER AFTER THINKING**

Fair Shares is a basic standard of life for everyone. Since we can never have true dignity while any one of us is ill-treated, we need to provide for the security and physical safety of all the peoples of the earth.

We can never feel peace while someone at the table is unfairly disadvantaged; we need to create access to food, clean water, shelter and essential medical care for everyone.

This is all affordable and achievable today, just as it is within our capability to ensure access to education for everyone and, beyond that, the chance to find meaningful work. Delivering Fair Shares is essential if we are to be able to say to future generations that we recognised and met the enormous challenge of our age, saving the human race from itself.

what else does this require ?

a foundation
of simple living values

This is the second element of a future worth choosing. Shared values are what will help different people from different cultures work together. Choosing these is easy; the same **living values** have been spoken of throughout history. In every tongue, in every tribe, on every continent, in every holy book and every political constitution, the wishes of every generation are the same. ◉

peace, justice, freedom, unity, truth, love

The future we want must always be visible in the methods we choose to achieve it. We cannot fight our way to peace, nor wait until we arrive to adopt the other values, we must act them out on the journey.

Our challenge is to learn to live by these values, so that
AS INDIVIDUALS we act peacefully and respect the equality of everyone in the choices we make every day.
AS COMMUNITIES we nurture our youngest, care for our eldest and provide for those in need.
IN COMMERCE we remake business to increase the general well-being of humankind through service, creativity and endeavour within an ethical framework.
AS NATIONS we cooperate rather than compete with other nations so as to provide for all the citizens of the world.

AS HUMANKIND we see our interdependence as more important than our independence and value the natural environment in which we co-exist with all other life forms.

Living these values can transform our lives: we will actually begin to live a **future worth choosing** now!

> Values are not just words, values are what we live by. They're about the causes that we champion and the people we fight for.
> **John Kerry**

what else do we need . . .

In balance with the natural world

In the early 50's, the Dayak people of Borneo suffered a malarial outbreak. The World Health Organisation (WHO) sprayed large amounts of DDT to kill the mosquitoes that carried the malaria. The mosquitoes died, the malaria declined, but there were unexpected side effects. The first was that the rooves of the people's houses began to fall on their heads: the DDT had also killed parasitic wasp that had previously controlled thatch-eating caterpillars. Worse, the DDT-poisoned insects were eaten by geckoes, which were eaten by cats. The cats started to die, the rats flourished, and the people were threatened by outbreaks of typhus and plague. To cope with these problems, which it had itself created, the WHO was obliged to parachute 14,000 live cats into Borneo. Operation Cat Drop, now almost forgotten at the WHO, is a graphic illustration of the interconnectedness of life, and how little we seem to understand of this.

Have we become accustomed to viewing other life forms as subordinate to human life? The cute and photogenic ones are lucky, the others might just be our next take-away meal or raw material for some other need. Do we really question our relationship with the rest of the natural world?

On this amazing planet there are millions of life forms alive and inter-connected; we are just one of them. We exist within a web that links us to the mosquito, the thatch-eating caterpillar, the gecko, the cat and the rat. The interdependencies within this web are too complex to map.

A Future Worth Choosing is impossible without the third element of protection for the living world; let's call this **Respect for Gaia.** We need a healthy biosphere to support human life, this alone is sufficient cause for us to respect and protect the planet. But our relationship with Gaia runs deeper than that; it is a primal connection and a fundamental interdependence. So we want to build a future that respects and protects that bond too and encourages reverence for the natural world.

Gaia, *n.* goddess of the earth whose body is the entire Earth, thought of as the Great Mother of all living things: in modern science, refers to the biosphere of the Earth considered to be a single living organism [from Greek mythology].

Whatever you can do,
or dream you can do
begin it.
Boldness has genius,
power and magic in it.
Begin it now.

Goethe

1990

2000

The ultimate test of a moral society is the kind
of world that it leaves to its children.

Dietrich Bonhoeffer

A world
for future generations

sustainable indefinitely   sustainable indefinitely   sustainable indefinitely   sustainable indefinitely   sustainable indefinitely

It has suddenly become very apparent that we are living well beyond our means, our savings are spent and the bank is nearly empty. We will reach the end of our resources with catastrophic results for human life unless we have a complete shift in our thinking.

The last element of the Future Worth Choosing is **Ever After Thinking**; developing our ability to live in harmony with our planet home indefinitely. We will relearn how to treat the world's finite reserves and renewable resources to ensure that children of every future generation can have their needs met in full. **Ever After Thinking** requires a significant shift in thought towards:

ABUNDANCE   our needs will be met somehow
POSSIBILITY   we will find a way
CO-OPERATION working together for the common good
and away from the deeply ingrained mindsets of:

SCARCITY   there isn't enough to go around
COMPETITION   it's a dog-eat-dog world

This will take us from ownership to stewardship; a world which we loan from our children, rather than inherit from our parents.

We must convince each generation that they are transient passengers on this planet earth. It does not belong to them. They are not free to doom generations yet unborn. They are not at liberty to erase humanity's past nor dim its future.
Bernard Lown and Evjueni Chazov

Sustainable, *adj.* meeting the needs of the present without compromising the ability of future generations to meet their own needs.

so can we create the world we want ?

Living
Happily
Ever After

**** YOUR PLANET NEEDS YOU ****

Fair Shares
+ Living Values
+ Respect for Gaia
+ Ever After Thinking

= A Future Worth Choosing

Thankyou for your concern
please call again

**** YOUR PLANET NEEDS YOU ****

A Future Worth Choosing is the vision of the continuation of human life on Earth that we must hold on to, whatever the challenges we see and however distant this future might appear to us today. The great achievements of human history have demonstrated our endeavour, creativity and capacity to survive threats of every kind. Right now we need to use these qualities in urgent and determined action to stave off catastrophe and realise this vision.

Already millions of people around the world have enlisted in this great calling, through action in their own lives and a host of wonderful initiatives. You are part of that number. With each individual who steps into greater awareness and action we all move closer to the **Future Worth Choosing**. The speed with which we arrive in that future depends on the speed of the spread of this idea; it is an idea that cannot be resisted, an idea whose time has come. ● We will see how that bold statement can be justified as we continue.

An invasion of ideas can be resisted, but not an idea whose time has come.
Victor Hugo

Our ideals, laws and customs should be based on the proposition that each generation, in turn, becomes the custodian rather than the absolute owner of our resources and each generation has the obligation to pass this inheritance on to the future.
Charles A. Lindbergh

how we shape the world

Extract + Mine +Drill + Dredge + Dig + Trawl + Chop + Strip + Refine + Smelt + Mould + Press + Assemble

our way of life shapes the world

When Henry
Ford and others first proposed the
automobile for a mass market, commentators
remarked with incredulity that this would require a
massive web of tarmac to be laid across the country with petrol
sales points built every few miles, surely impossible.
A hundred years later every country in the developed world has tarmac
laid and pumps primed: the motorcar has shaped the world.
We call this progress, but when we take into account the 812 hours spent every
year earning the money to buy and keep a car plus the time spent using it and the
distance travelled each year our average speed is less than that of a bicycle! 🌐
This is only one of the more obvious examples of how we have fashioned the
world to support our way of life. Elsewhere we extract and convert the materials
of the natural world into our chemicals and raw materials, and eventually into
homes and computers and foodstuffs and fabrics and gadgets, and yes, more
cars. Our appetites drive the industrial machine on its path around the
earth, this path has become a trail of destruction. So quite clearly one of
the major factors shaping the natural world is how we choose to live.
The limits to this impact are no longer those of what is possible. We
have the technology to do anything on which we focus our
considerable energy and resources. It is the limits of our
appetite for consumption that will ultimately determine
the fate of the human race and the condition of
our   precious   home,   Planet
Earth

our way of life shapes the world

+ Stitch + Process + Package + Box + Shrink wrap + Distribute + Ship + Buy + Consume = Time Bomb

how we live every day shapes the world that we live in and . . .

You make me sick, I will kill you

our th**o**ughts

The quest of Dr Masaru Emoto, a Japanese scientist, to discover the mystery of water involved research around the planet. He realised that, in the frozen crystal form, water shows us its true nature and he has used this to demonstrate a remarkable phenomenon. Dr Emoto has proved that human thoughts affect physical reality: they literally shape the world. When samples of water are exposed to our thoughts, in spoken or written form, the crystal shape of water changes. Both prayer and music have also been shown to cause water to change its expression. **This is the Power of Thought.**

Love and Thanks

also shape the world

We've seen how the way we choose to live is leaving an indelible print on our planet. We also need to recognise that thoughts are a dynamic force for shaping our world.

> Your consciousness influences others around you. It influences material properties. It influences your future. You are co-creating your future.
> **William Tiller**

We know thought precedes action, guiding what we do. We also know that thoughts are powerful enough to affect our health, Doctors have recognised this for centuries. The simple belief in a treatment being effective is enough to ensure a cure. Pills with no pharmaceutical ingredient work when the patient believes they will.

Thought also has the power to transform material at the molecular level: we now know this through the astonishing work of Dr Emoto.

The photographs above show the beautiful crystal shape of water labelled with the words, **"Love and Thanks."**

The image on the facing page shows very different water crystals from a sample labelled **"You make me sick, I will kill you."**

So, have no doubt, every thought we choose also leaves its own indelible print. Now we need to identify the dominant thought patterns that currently hold sway in the human mind, and see the impact that these have on our behaviour and our world.

lets look at this . . .

EXCESS

One of the thoughts which shapes the world is excess (and boy, do we do excess)

It all started quite innocently. Like a child in a sweet shop we wanted to try a bit of everything on offer. It was exciting at first, but now it seems we are locked in the shop with more than enough pocket money and an inexhaustible supply of candy. We were lured into the shop in the first place by the sales messages; 'Go on treat yourself', 'It's a bargain', 'Buy one get one free'. Everyone else was shopping anyway and we didn't want to be left out or look poor. More subtle messages followed: 'Don't be seen with yesterday's candy, new Candy-Max now available' and the advertising that told us we could be cool, glamorous, like a celebrity, if only we got the right candy. It started to seem the more we could buy, and be seen to buy, the better person we would become.

EXCEPT OF COURSE *that all of these messages play on our lowest instincts*
EXCEPT OF COURSE *the candy is actually the* STUFF *we buy to support our comfortable lives*
EXCEPT OF COURSE *no amount of* STUFF *can actually make us happy*
EXCEPT OF COURSE *other people have to starve so we can gorge on this* STUFF
EXCEPT OF COURSE *we are raping the planet to extract the resources to make this* STUFF*, and*
EXCEPT OF COURSE *the shop is not locked, the key that gets us out is restraint, moderation, and the magic word,* **ENOUGH**

CONSUMER JARGON

Marketing, *n.* historically the process of identifying and satisfying customer needs profitably; in common usage persuading gullible consumers to purchase unnecessary new products [see also pick-up trucks, plug-in air fresheners, packaged grated cheese.]
Stuff, *n.* material goods which serve no long-term purpose except in the temporary pleasure felt in the acquisition : as in "you can never have enough stuff."
Excess, *n.* a polite word for greed

TRUE or FALSE?

Aristotle used to walk through the market of Athens every day without buying. When asked why he replied, "To better understand the difference between my needs and my wants."

Our thoughts of excess have taken us so far beyond our needs into our wants that we ignore the true and terrifying cost of feeding our habit and we have almost lost sight of a simple truth: it doesn't have to be this way.

we can live lightly on the planet if we choose

...and round it goes again, angry thoughts and an angry world, and round again, violent thoughts and a world of war and terror, and round again......like chicken and egg in a ceaseless cycle, never sure which comes first ....

ANGER

What makes you angry?

It doesn't take much to make us angry

In a world getting ever faster
When we're busy, busy, busy
Where it's each for their own, no-one else will look out for us
With news media bringing bad and depressing news 24/7
Where there is always someone else to blame
Where our expectations are raised so high, so frequently
Where the Living Values seem to take a daily battering

How easy it is in these circumstances to think

FRUSTRATION ...... it doesn't seem fair
EXASPERATION .... if only other people would do it right
ANGER .... just bl**dy angry
REVENGE .... we're not going to let them get away with it

Is it surprising that Hollywood plays back to us an obsession with violence and retribution, or that the most popular genre of kids' computer games centre on mutilation and death? And it doesn't have to be this way.

Programs designed for children are 5 to 6 times more violent than adult TV and average viewing means kids see about 10,000 television rapes, assaults, and murders each year.

Hundreds of studies of the effects of TV violence on children and teenagers have found that children may:
• become "immune" to the horror of violence
• gradually accept violence as a way to solve problems
• imitate the violence they observe on television

American Academy of Child and Adolescent Psychiatry

So long as governments set the example of killing their enemies, private individuals will occasionally kill theirs.
Elbert Hubbard

we can check out of Anger, destination peace and tolerance, any time we choose

FEAR

Be afraid: be very afraid!

"It's a jungle out there", "a rat race", "life ain't easy", "it's a struggle"; we live with all of these metaphors in which threat and risk lurk around every corner. And however we may pretend otherwise, deep down we have absorbed that fear, we are afraid. 🕸

It becomes

FEAR of the dark
FEAR of spiders
FEAR of pain
FEAR of being hurt
FEAR of being alone
FEAR of being trapped
FEAR of not being good enough
FEAR of being too good
FEAR of terrorism
FEAR of death

This fear is like an imbalance at the very centre of our being; it throws everything else out of kilter. Psychologically it becomes the root of our dysfunction, of all our destructive emotions; it sabotages our success and contaminates our relationships; it is the root of greed, anger, prejudice and envy. Fear drives out the possibility of love and compassion and acceptance.

Some of our fears are well founded and physiologically useful, but some are simply **F**alse **E**motion **A**ppearing **R**eal. The key to freedom from fear is to be able to distinguish the latter and loosen the grip they have had on our lives. 🕸

The hens they all cackle, the roosters all beg,
But I will not hatch, I will not hatch.
For I hear all the talk of pollution and war.
As the people all shout and the airplane roar,
So I'm staying in here where it's safe and it's warm,
And I WILL NOT HATCH!
Shel Silverstein

Living in fear we throw up barriers to keep ourselves separate and safe; we can see this in our own lives and on the global stage too. As nations we barricade ourselves behind borders with our weapons armed and ready to fire at a hostile world. Once again the prevailing culture of our times influences our thinking, and once again we see how our thinking reinforces and shapes that culture.

LOVE

Our positive thoughts can shape the world too

We've seen people and situations transformed when we act in love or kindness. We've also been moved when other people have acted toward us from these same thoughts. The power of love face-to-face is proven.

These same thoughts can affect our collective culture on occasions like religious festivals or national sporting triumph when goodwill permeates the way we interact with each other.

A few very special moments have given us a glimpse of this power acting globally:

Nelson Mandela's release from prison and election into office represented the end of an oppression that had seemed unbreakable, sparking a feeling of joy and optimism everywhere. The world felt lighter for a while.

The fall of the Berlin Wall was broadcast live all around the world, again showing that 'impossible' situations can be transformed, releasing a sense of hope for untold millions.

The tsunami of 2005 triggered waves of compassion that surged around the globe. The magnitude of our individual response embarrassed governments to rethink the depth of their own response. In that very moment our positive thoughts shaped the world.

Imagine the impact when we can harness thoughts as powerful as these.

> All that we are is the result of what we have thought. If a man speaks or acts with an evil thought, pain follows him. If a man speaks or acts with a pure thought, happiness follows him, like a shadow that never leaves him.
> **Buddha**

> We look forward to the time when the power to love will replace the love of power. Then will our world know the blessings of peace.
> **William Ewart Gladstone**

The world as a mirror

The world as a mirror

Yes, our thoughts shape the world, for good or for ill. And the dominant thoughts of our culture shape our individual thoughts and behaviour, it's a circle round and round. So the world acts as a giant mirror reflecting our thoughts back to us.

This is true for us individually: our thinking is reflected back to us by the quality of our relationships, and the degree of fitness and peace of mind that we have. Sobering but true.

Collectively the reality of the world in the early days of the 21st century is a perfect reflection of the combined thinking of the human race. We have exactly the level of peace and happiness that matches our thinking: we have an environment that reflects our degree of love for it: we have business systems and ethics that echo our priorities: we have the political systems and leaders that our collective awareness deserves.

so let's have a look in the mirror

CHAPTER THREE

VGA 4.1mm 1:2.8

4x Digital Zoom

take a closer look
at yourself...

a snapshot of our world

A World **of grotesque injustice**

Half the people in the world live on **less than $2 a day**

This is less than the price of a cup of coffee in a high street coffee shop. In direct comparision, consider that every European farmer receives from the European Commission $2.20 per day for every cow in the herd! Do we value cows more than humans? 🌐

This happens because our governments stack the deck when we trade with the third world. We subsidise our own industries to protect our own national interests and then force developing countries to allow subsidised goods into their own markets. We call it 'free trade' and tell them to like it or lump it. If they don't accept the rules, they don't get the aid.

This means imported frozen chicken parts from Europe and USA are being sold in African countries for one third of the price of local poultry. The local chicken farmer simply can't compete, many simply give up and turn to handouts. In a country of 18 million people like Ghana only one in ten chickens sold are reared in the country, and the environment groans ever louder as we ship frozen chicken around the world. It's nuts!

Who makes these rules?

Who makes these rules? Step forward the World Bank and the International Monetary Fund who do this on behalf of our governments. It gets worse: managers from our multi-national companies staff the committees that draft these rules. So the very people who stand to gain most from the rules get to write them.

Common sense, justice and the chicken farmer all fall victim to the world trade system, which is designed to guarantee that the rich get richer at the expense of the poor getting poorer. In our name!

> The international trading system was devised by the rich to suit their needs; it ignores those of the poor.
> **Pope Paul VI**

> I was wrong: free market trade policies hurt the poor…the rules of international trade are rigged against the poorest countries.
> **Stephen Byers, speaking as former Trade and Industry Secretary, UK**

**Every day
3 billion human beings**
live on less than the price of
a skinny latte 🌐

**The 3 richest people
in the world**
control more wealth than
600 000 000 people
in the poorest countries
on earth 🌐

**For every $1
we provide in aid**
we rob the developing nations
of $2 through our scandalous
trade rules 🌐

**The USA spends more money
every year** building prisons
than schools 🌐

**80 of the poorest countries in
the world** are poorer now than
they were 20 years ago 🌐

how does this make you feel ?

A World **of unimaginable suffering**

67 people are dying of poverty related conditions
as you read this page ⊕

For as long as we tolerate billions of people living in poverty, there will be an inevitable death toll. This currently stands at 50 000 each day, every one of them someone's daughter, someone's son ......
today, and tomorrow ......
and the day after ......
and the day after that ......

Nothing condemns us more completely than this treatment of the poor and needy in our midst, because we could put an end to this right now if we only cared enough.

For an estimated $19 bn per year we could end starvation and malnutrition everywhere, but we don't.

And we do spend $47 bn every year on ice cream. Choc ice anyone?

When I feed the poor I am called a saint, when I ask why the poor are poor I am called a communist.
Joseph Rowntree

The day that hunger is eradicated from the earth, there will be the greatest spiritual explosion the world has ever known. Humanity cannot imagine the joy that will burst into the world on the day of that great revolution.
Fredrico Garcia Lorca

That's somebody's daughter, somebody's son, every three seconds

A World **of perverted priorities**

Consider this: one in five of the world's children get no schooling whatsoever.
And: only one in five of the children who do get to primary school continue into education in their teenage years.
Now Consider: worldwide we spend $1 trillion a year on weapons to kill each other and destroy the world. ⬤

If we choose education as the weapon to change the world it will only take an extra $10 billion each year to provide primary education for every child

the equivalent of just three and a half days spend on arms. ⬤

Shocking Fact 1
We have legitimised this as a business; we allow our governments, corporations and ourselves to make money from selling ways to kill people.

Shocking Fact 2
Encouraged and enabled by this trade there are now more than 30 armed conflicts around the world and roughly one third of the world's population is at war. ⬤

Every gun that is made, every warship launched, every rocket fired signifies, in the final sense, a theft from those who hunger and are not fed, those who are cold and are not clothed. [The world] is spending the sweat of its laborers, the genius of its scientists, the hopes of its children...
President Dwight Eisenhower

[Education is] the means by which men and women deal critically and creatively with reality and discover how to participate in the transformation of their world.
Paulo Freire

IN THE FACE OF THIS INJUSTICE AND SUFFERING
EDUCATION
IS THE MOST POWERFUL WEAPON
WHICH YOU CAN USE
TO CHANGE THE WORLD.
Nelson Mandela
The Think TANK
The Think TANK
The
YPNY
CHOOSE YOUR WEAPONS
Think

A World **of mindless devastation**

When humankind was solely reliant on sunlight to grow the food we ate, the Earth supported one billion people. 150 years ago we learned to use our reserves of fossil fuel. Since then we have been able to farm more land more intensively and our population has shot up to $6\frac{1}{2}$ billion. In the process our whole way of life has industrialised; we have become 'addicted to oil'. There is no firm agreement about exactly how much oil and gas remain but with an accelerating rate of usage, we're unlikely to outlast this century: our orgy of consumption will last no more than 250 years from the beginning of the Industrial Revolution until the fossil fuel tank is empty. And without these reserves we only have today's sunlight to support the extra five billion people. ⊛

We are exhausting the earth's supply of **Fossil Fuel** with no thought for the needs of our children.

ditto	**Rainforest,** between 20 and 40 years to say our goodbyes ⊛
ditto	**Atlantic Cod,** stocks collapsed and not recovering ⊛
ditto	**Grain,** harvest less than consumption globally for 4th year in a row ⊛
ditto	**Fresh Water,** two-thirds of all people in severe shortage by 2025 ⊛
ditto	**Top soil,** agricultural land area size of China at 'very high risk' of human induced desertification ⊛
ditto	**Polar Ice Cap,** 20% gone in the last 25 years ⊛

This mass extinction is the fastest in Earth's 4.5-billion-year history and, unlike prior extinctions, is mainly the result of human activity and not of natural phenomena.
American Museum of Natural History

If we live as if it matters and it doesn't matter, it doesn't matter. If we live as if it doesn't matter and it matters, then it matters.
Professor Norman Myers

it took the planet!

70 Million Years

to build it's stock of!

FOSSIL FUELS

FACTORY

INDUSTRY

oh no!

in 50 YEARS

they will all be!

GONE

A World **of enormous uncertainty**

Or is it? Here are five perspectives on our climate challenge

Serious changes

Independent scientific opinion is all but unanimous; climate change is real and we are the major cause. Its implications go way beyond global warming: sea level rise, environmental chaos, unstable weather patterns and disruption to the food chain are inevitable. ❀

Past the tipping point

When Arctic sea ice fails to reform in the winter and the frozen tundra of Siberia starts to thaw there is reason to believe the rate of warming will only accelerate. Perhaps we can no longer avoid these changes, merely minimise them through prudent action. ❀

Our greatest oppportunity

Evolutionary biologist Elisabet Sahtouris wonders whether global warming is nature's lesson for us now, and poses the interesting question whether this can be the crisis that finally drives us to global cooperation and sustainability. ❀

And still they deny it

The loudest voices still arguing the human cause of climate change are far from independent. Often it is industry lobby groups which fund the activities and research of those who seek to confuse and cloud the issue. *He who pays the piper calls the tune!* ❀

Let's plan

Its time to turn our attention to the difficult questions: How will we cope with millions of people displaced by sea water in Bangladesh, the Thames Estuary or Manhattan? How will we protect our agriculture from temperature effects and water shortage? How will we adapt our lifestyles to head off the worst possible scenarios?

It is important, vital even, that we sift through these perspectives to find quick and appropriate responses to this climate challenge. We will be defined for posterity by the choices that we make right now.

Vorsorgeprinzip, *n.* German word, the precautionary principle which advises that we take action before we have scientific proof of the need to act, on the grounds that delay or inaction might ultimately be more costly to society and nature and, longer term, selfish and unfair to future generations. [see also: Better Safe than Sorry.]

A World **of hopefulness**

We are awakening from this crazy, shortsighted dream in ever growing numbers. Our wake-up calls are the very problems we've catalogued and every natural disaster and man-made horror we experience. People all over the world are beginning to realise we can build a new and different world. This is no longer a fringe of radical intellectuals, single-issue activists and extreme environmentalists; we are ordinary folk who understand this is the defining challenge of our age.

There is hope in the number of people who are now prepared to take action in response. And there is hope in the fabulous and creative ideas that are arising to help tackle this need.

New patterns of thinking are emerging; awareness of our environment has never been higher; millions take to streets around the world calling for peace; there is an upsurge of interest in matters of the spirit; we begin to re-evaluate our lifestyle. Green and simple living hasn't yet replaced conspicuous consumption, but there are signs that the stranglehold of materialism is loosening its grip in the west.

Gathering the critical mass

In 1952, on the island of Koshima, scientists were providing monkeys with sweet potatoes dropped in the sand. The monkeys liked the taste of the raw potatoes, but found the sand unpleasant. One monkey learned to wash the potatoes in a nearby stream. She taught this trick to her mother and playmates and over the next 6 years all the young monkeys and some adults learned too. Other adults kept eating the dirty sweet potatoes.

Then something startling took place. Let's suppose one morning there were 99 monkeys on Koshima Island who had learned to wash their sweet potatoes. Let's further suppose that later that morning, the 100th monkey learned to wash potatoes.

Then it happened!

By that evening almost everyone in the tribe was washing sweet potatoes before eating them; and the behaviour soon jumped over the sea, colonies of monkeys on other islands and the mainland began to do the same. *The added energy of this hundredth monkey somehow created an ideological breakthrough.* 🐵

Thus, when a certain critical number achieves an awareness, this new awareness may be communicated from mind to mind. This is the same moment Malcolm Gladwell calls the Tipping Point, the moment of critical mass, the threshold where radical change on an enormous scale is more than a possibility. It becomes a certainty. 🐵

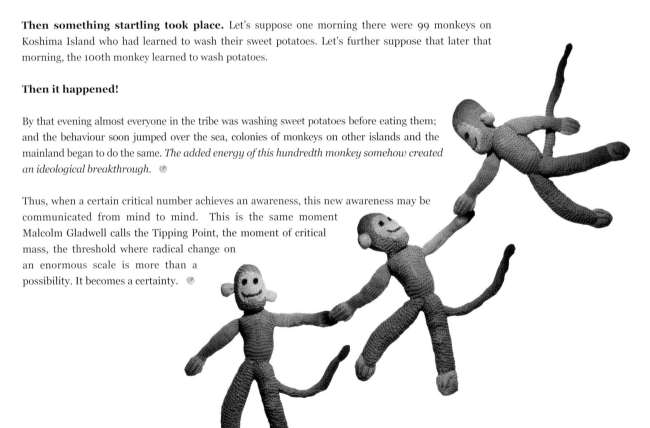

the call

We are either part of the problem . . .

We can no longer claim ignorance. We know beyond doubt that we are responsible for the state of our world, we know what a mess we are making. We know that individually we are inextricably linked into this through our actions and our awareness; all of which leaves us just two choices; we are part of the problem or part of the solution.

Sometimes it falls upon a generation to be great. You can be that great generation. Let your greatness b l o s s o m . Of course the task will not be easy. But not to do this would be a crime against humanity, against which I ask all humanity now to rise up. **Nelson Mandela.** You can't rely on governments to solve the world's environmental problems. **Al Gore.** Never doubt that a small group of thoughtful, committed citizens can change the world. Indeed, it's the only thing that ever has. **Margaret Mead.** There are no passengers on Spaceship Earth. We are all crew. **M a r s h a l l McCluhan.**

And so to work...

We are the solution. Changing the world starts with us and involves the two ways in which we are constantly shaping the world. **Our Way of Life and Our Thoughts.**

This is how we can respond, this how we can step into our response - ability for the world. We can make an immediate impact through our way of life and through simple Action: this is the outward journey. The inward journey is where we change ourselves, our thoughts and our Awareness.

We cannot do one without the other, Action without a shift in personal Awareness will be short-lived and of limited impact. And a change in our Awareness will always affect the Action we choose to take in the world.

We create the circumstances to transform the world we live in when we tread both paths together. When we do this we act as a Voice of the Future.

Voice of the Future, *n.* a person prepared to act for a better world through their own thought and deed
[for fuller details visit **www.yourplanetneedsyou.org** to add your name to the global list of these Voices]

How wonderful it is that nobody need wait a single moment before starting to improve the world.
Anne Frank

We must be the change we want to see in the world.
Mahatma Gandhi

Our thoughts and actions define the world for our children.
Morel Fourman

what we can do

Live lightly on the planet

We each leave our own personal impact on Planet Earth. This is a direct measure of all of the resources we use and the waste we create in our way of life. Our 'footprint' reflects what we eat, buy and wear, how and where we travel, where and how we live, in short, every aspect of our standard of living. Behind that, and unseen to us, it measures the energy and waste involved at every stage of growing, converting and transporting everything that we consume. As a **Voice of the Future** the wonderful opportunity we have is to make an immediate difference to our effect on the environment.

Live Lightly on the Planet

means reducing our personal footprint to as close to zero as we reasonably can

Live Lightly on the Planet

means consuming only our share of Earth's resources so that every other human being can have their fair share too

Live Lightly on the Planet

means finding a contentment dependent on quality of life, rather than the hollow fix afforded by our standard of living

Living lightly is a vital and worthy goal as we progress toward a Future Worth Choosing. It is the common-sense response to our over-use of the environment; it is the compassionate response to the world's inequality; it is the personally liberating response to our culture of wanting ever more, bigger and better.

Why

Mankind's collective footprint more than doubled in the last 40 years and together we now consume the resources of more than one earth-sized planet.

But if we all lived as the Americans live we would need an astonishing 6 planets for our needs. And even if the entire population of the world lived more modestly to a UK standard of living we would need 3 planets. [According to astronomers, there is still only one Planet Earth in view.]

Zero footprint is the target where we consume only within Earth's natural capacity for replenishment and leave no lasting damage or depletion on the earth

Luxurious living is an impossible proposition for any society as a whole. And when there is no limit to luxury, where shall we stop? Plain living and high thinking is the ideal that has been placed before us. The vast majority recognise its truth, but are unable to get there because of human frailty.
Mahatma Gandhi

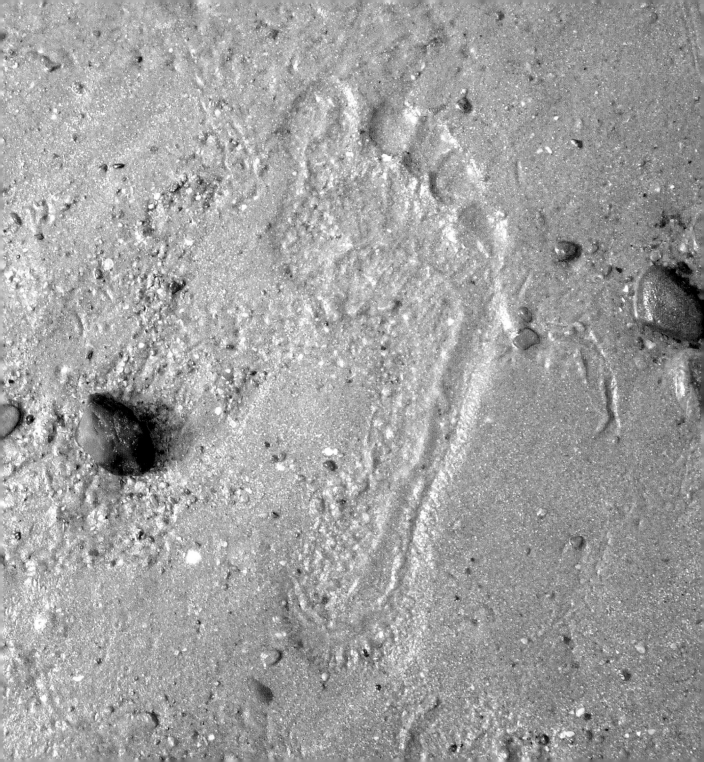

The mantra for Reducing our Footprint is
Reduce, Reuse, Recycle

Reduce.......where we can (cut down on what we use)   **reduced** where we can reduce

- BUY LESS
- GO WITHOUT
- USE IT TILL IT WEARS OUT
- BUY SECOND HAND
- BUY RECYCLED

- AVOID DISPOSABLE GOODS
- DECLINE OR RETURN PACKAGING
- REFILL
- BUY IN BULK, USE SPARINGLY
- LIVE SIMPLY

Reuse where goods can be **Reused** in their existing form by someone

- REPAIR
- REINVENT
- DONATE
- SELL

or ask somebody you know if they would like it
or ask somebody if they know somebody who would like it
or ask somebody if they know somebody who knows somebody who would like it

Recycle where goods can be **Recycled** into new goods

- USE LOCAL AMENITIES TO THE MAX
- SEPARATE
- COMPOST
- AND BUY RECYCLED PRODUCTS

There are fantastic resources available to help us Live Lightly, some are listed in the Appendices.
There are other great books and lots of ideas online too.

Let's **Get Informed;** we can't make a difference if we don't know where we are Living Heavily.

enough, *adj.*
sufficient to meet a need or satisfy a desire: adequate.

think
RRR
before you shop

A avoid aerosols: **B** banish batteries [*the disposable ones*]: **C** can cans [*buy bulk or fresh wherever possible*]: **D** don't do disposables [*cameras/nappies/pens*]: **E** eat everything and eliminate excess [*don't waste food before or after its cooked*]: **F** forego foil: **G** go green in the garden [*grow your own and avoid inorganic anything*]: **H** hire handiwork help [*don't just buy tools, share, borrow, lend, pool or swap*]: **I** improve information [*find out where to recycle aluminium, glass, batteries, mobiles, inkjets etc*]: **J** jumble your junk: **K** KISS [*keep it simple and sustainable*]: **L** love low-energy light-bulbs: **M** moderation: **N** natural not nylon [*avoid synthetics wherever possible*]: **O** order organic: **P** prevent proliferation of plastic packaging: **Q** question quantity: **R** reduce, reuse, recycle: **S** send second-hand stuff to someone: **T** trade toddlers toys: **U** use underlay [*and all other forms of insulation*]: **V** value vests [*and turn the central heating down 1 degree*]: **W** walk [*don't drive*]: **X** x-tract [*separate anything recyclable from your office waste too*]: **Y** yes [*we can do it*]: **Z** zero [*the target footprint*]

Make your Money
Make a Difference

Money is energy. It supports and reinforces wherever it flows, and **we** have a choice about how **we** use that energy and where **we** use our money. **We** shape the world through **how we spend our money.**

We can use our money in the most powerful way possible as compassionate, ethical consumers and as generous philanthropists too.

Making your Money Make a Difference
means supporting the people, practices and products which are aligned with our goal of a Future Worth Choosing

Making your Money Make a Difference
means boycotting the people, practices and products which reinforce and exploit the limited world we've got now

Making your Money Make a Difference
means using disposable income to support charities and good causes for which we have passion

Money talks, and business listens very attentively to how we use it. People power has been demonstrated over and over; let's harness it to fund a Future Worth Choosing.

£12.50 in every £100 retail spend in the UK goes to Tesco
$9 in every $100 in the USA to Wal-Mart
Imagine how much difference we can make by lobbying
these retailers

Why

An ordinary week's expenditure in the developed world might be supporting

Child labour - *cheap clothing*
Rain Forest clearing - *to graze cattle for burger beef*
Unfair international trade rules - *most multi-nationals are deeply involved in the World Trade Organisation*
Arms Sales - *most governments use tax income to subsidise this trade*
Animal Testing - *make-up and household cleaners*
Waste and Pollution - *all the unnecessary packaging wrapped around what we buy*

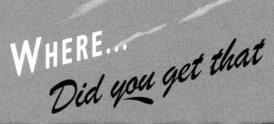

WHERE...
Did you get that
STRAWBERRY?

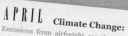

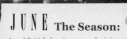

Power **Spending**

The basis of ethical consumption is information. We need to know about the total impact of the products we might buy or the organisations selling to us in order to make ethical choices.

What's ethical is a personal choice too, all our choices will be slightly different. Here are a few to consider

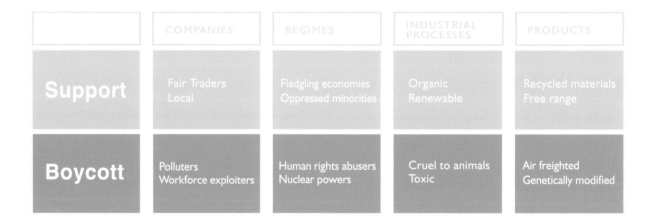

	COMPANIES	REGIMES	INDUSTRIAL PROCESSES	PRODUCTS
Support	Fair Traders Local	Fledgling economies Oppressed minorities	Organic Renewable	Recycled materials Free range
Boycott	Polluters Workforce exploiters	Human rights abusers Nuclear powers	Cruel to animals Toxic	Air freighted Genetically modified

To make our economic choices even more powerful we can tell the suppliers what we are doing and why. We can write or speak to the people we support and tell them. Go on, make their day! And write to those we boycott too; tell 'em why. It doubles the impact of our action.

And we have choices with our discretionary spending too. We can use our surplus income for the good of others as well as ourselves, supporting any of the countless charities and organisations that are working so hard to fashion a Future Worth Choosing.

penny on...poverty gone!™ ©

Be of **Service**

Serving gives us the opportunity to help someone else in need of assistance. We can use our time, our energy or maybe some particular skills we have to good effect.
It makes an immediate and positive difference in the world.

Volunteering gives an immediate payoff to us in the pride and satisfaction of helping. The sense of accomplishing something worthwhile is its own reward. As a **Voice of the Future** we can make a difference on our own doorstep or in a project we feel passionate about anywhere in the world.

Be of Service
means finding practical ways to give our time, energy or expertise to organisations doing good in the world

Be of Service
means caring for other people, or our community, or our environment or all of them

Be of Service
means doing something for nothing

When we act together in service to the needy or for the greater good we unlock a tremendous power that is seldom tapped in the conventional trade of time-for-money. We automatically add to the flow of goodwill and hope in the world.

Why

Service is the opportunity to give something back, and to express our innate humanity, and.....
Existing research indicates that volunteering can improve self-esteem, reduce heart rates and blood pressure, increase endorphin production, enhance immune systems, buffer the impact of stress, and combat social isolation.

I don't know what your destiny will be, but one thing I do know: the only ones among you who will be really happy are those who have sought and found how to serve.
Albert Schweitzer

Service is the
rent we pay to be
living. It is the
very purpose of
life and not something
you do in your
spare time.
Marion Wright Edelman

VOLUNTEERS WANTED

The Youth Club needs
adults, any age, to help
run after-school homework
club 3.30 – 5.00 weekdays
Call Linda 675409

A society grows great
when old men plant trees
whose shade they know
they shall never sit in.
GREEK PROVERB.

Your local
Community
Association
urgently needs
a
Treasurer.
Common sense +
willingness are all
that is required.
Call Sandy
842906

Jumble Sale

Saturday 11th June – 2pm
Church Hall   Helpers Wanted
Proceeds to Mother + Toddler Group

Illustrated Talk

I've just got back from a
year of service in a school
for disadvantaged kids in the
Peruvian Andes. Come and
hear about it at the Church Hall
Thursday 16th June 7.30 pm
ENTRY FREE

PENSIONER NEEDS HELP WITH
OVERGROWN GARDEN
PLEASE CALL AT MY HOUSE
NUMBER 22 ELM ROAD
(TEA AND CAKES) FOR HELPERS

Everybody can be great...
because anybody can serve.
You don't have to have a
college degree to serve. You don't
have to make your subject + verb
agree to serve. You only need
a heart full of grace, a soul
generated by love.
Martin Luther King

Stand up **Speak out**

Every point of view counts and every voice counts. Democracy relies upon us all **speaking truth to power** so the decision-makers of the day hear our views and see the world through our eyes.

We need to be prepared to say clearly, loudly and constructively that we passionately believe in a different and better way of life. **We are Voices of the Future.**

Stand Up, Speak Out
starts with taking a stand for a Future Worth Choosing, this alone creates the space in which it will happen

Stand Up Speak Out
means knowing your mind and being prepared to state a point of view, to take a stand for what you believe to be right and just

Stand Up Speak Out
means play your part in the democratic process by voting, marching, writing, lobbying, making our voice heard

Not only does every voice count but when we speak with one voice we will be an undeniable force for change, for fairness, for justice and peace. Our voice will call down the walls that separate us from each other and from the world we want. Our voice will usher in the Future Worth Choosing.

Why

A British Member of Parliament says 6 letters on a subject is evidence of significant concern amongst constituents. The British Broadcasting Corporation says that the same number of complaints, just 6, about a programme will be taken as serious feedback.

First they came for the Communists, but I was not a Communist so I did not speak out. Then they came for the Socialists and the Trade Unionists, but I was neither, so I did not speak out. Then they came for the Jews, but I was not a Jew so I did not speak out. And when they came for me, there was no one left to speak out for me. **Martin Niemoeller**

what do you stand for ?

Just **Shine**

What a wonderful force of positive energy we are in the world. We already know the power of positive thoughts when we are optimistic, helpful and encouraging to others; we know how good this makes others feel. So every day is a chance to shine and to see this light reflect back in other people.

Just Shine

starts with being constructive, always finding the good in people and situations, however difficult this might be. It means celebrating Possibility as well as Success; it means the glass is half-full

Just Shine

is role modelling the good humour, kindness and courtesy that we enjoy so much in other people

Just Shine

means being a source of love and encouragement in the world, leaving others feeling better than you found them

Imagine how far the ripple spreads when you smile or show a simple kindness to someone else. Imagine a room chock-full of smiles, a town brimful of kindness or a world overflowing with love.

Isn't that the Future Worth Choosing?

Why

We all know people who consistently makes us feel upbeat, and probably someone else who does the opposite – **which one are you?**

Reviewing recent research by psychologists, we have started to figure out what makes people happy.

The answer is simple: family, friends, meaningful activities, the ability to forgive and the opportunity to love.

and you can start it all with a smile

But sometimes... **it ain't so easy**

There are a few obstacles to navigate in our journey of social action. Whether we hear them from other people or in the excuses we make to ourselves, they seem to boil down to a few responses corresponding to some common states of mind.

I'M ALREADY DOING MY BIT	ALREADY ACTIVE
I WOULD BUT DON'T KNOW WHERE TO START	NEEDING HELP
THERE'S NOTHING I CAN DO	IMPOTENT
IT'S NOT MY PROBLEM	INDIFFERENT
I KNOW I SHOULDN'T DO THIS, BUT I LIKE IT	SEDUCED
THERE'S NO PROBLEM	IN DENIAL
WHAT PROBLEM?	IGNORANT

We might be caught in any one of these traps, maybe more than one. We could be simultaneously Already Active, recycling household waste, but In Denial, about our reliance on using the car, whilst Indifferent, about homeless people in our own neighbourhood, and happily seduced by another cheap flight for a weekend break.

This doesn't make us 'wrong' or 'bad' it simply highlights how much opportunity there is for us to make a difference. Instead of just trying harder to be more active, we need to start looking at our own awareness.

If you don't want to do something, one excuse is as good as another.
Yiddish Proverb

Difficulty is the excuse history never accepts.
Edward R. Murrow

on the one hand....

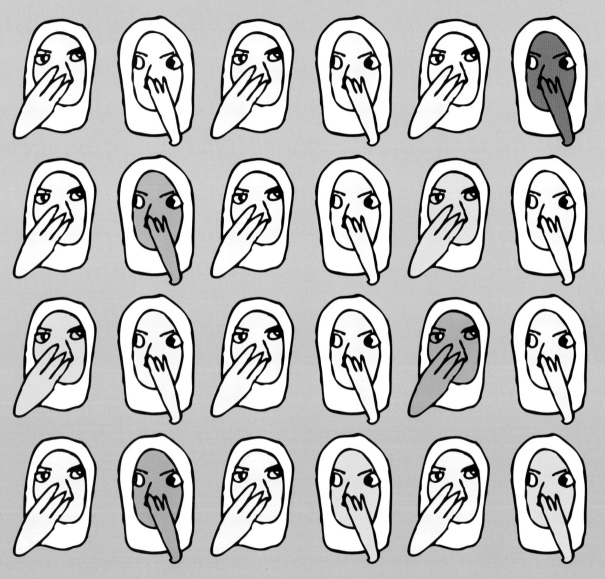

on the other hand....

Difference **through action**
We've looked at these five ways
to make a difference

Live Lightly on the Planet
Make your Money Make a Difference
Be of Service
Stand Up Speak Out
Just Shine

We can adopt these principals at home, with our families, at work or further afield in the communities where we live. And as well as this, to change the world we need to change the way we think, **and that's awareness.**

Each time a person stands up for an idea, or acts to improve the lot of others, or strikes out against injustice, he sends forth a tiny ripple of hope, and crossing each other from a million different centres of energy and daring, those ripples build a current that can sweep down the mightiest walls of oppression and resistance.
Robert Kennedy

If you get in touch with your Self you will experience a natural, spontaneous sense of responsibility.
Werner Erhard

so let's explore the Three Dimensions of Awareness

awareness

First being willing to **transform me**

To help the transformation in the world we need to look at transforming me. **This is the first dimension of awareness.**

Loving ourselves is fundamental. We can't love anyone or anything else more than we love ourselves. So the limit of the love, care and concern we can show for other people and for our environment lies in how much we love ourselves. When we love and accept ourselves more fully every one else benefits too, and we become more effective in the world.

Living authentically is living free of inhibition or constraint and living to our own truth. It sometimes means having the courage to avoid the easy, familiar or popular options to do what we know is right. Being authentic means discovering our true purpose, that sense of the greatest contribution we can make in the world. Being aligned with purpose puts our own unique talents in service for ourselves and for others, it unlocks the richest and most joyful life we can live. This is the second part of transforming ourselves.

Being ready to change and adapt is the third key, we have got to be willing to be work-in-progress, reflecting on where we are effective and where we are blocked. This is a continuing job.

Conscience is a great guide in this work; it's that inner voice which whispers in our ear, guiding us to stay on the right path. We can cultivate conscience simply by listening; the more we pay attention to it and allow it to guide our actions, the stronger it is. Then it will help us to be loving to ourselves, to find our purpose and to stay authentic on this inner journey.

Cowardice asks the question, "Is it safe?" Expediency asks the question, "Is it politic?" Vanity asks the question "Is it popular?" But conscience asks the question "Is it right?" And there comes a time when one must take a position that is neither safe, nor politic, nor popular but one must take it because one's conscience tells one that it is right.
Dr Martin Luther King

Conscience, *n.* the awareness of a moral or ethical aspect to one's conduct together with the urge to prefer right over wrong.

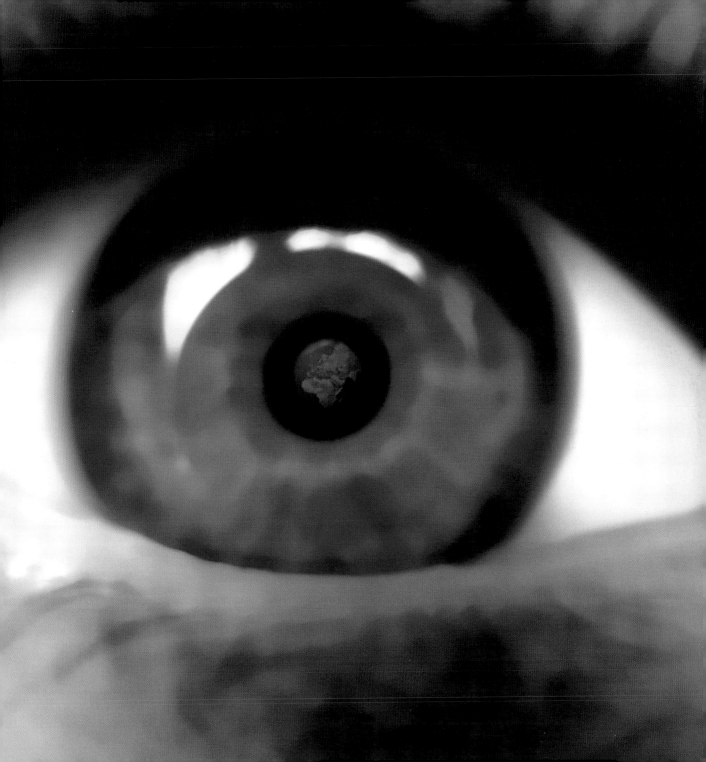

Being ONE **human family**

There are 6½ billion of us here on earth, all unique and all united by our common humanity. Beyond the differences of colour, tongue, religion or belief we share the same hopes and dreams, worries and fears; about ourselves, our own families and **our future.**

It's easy to feel a separation from other people in a world that encourages us to succeed as individuals. We can quickly become indifferent to the fate of people in far off countries or very different cultures. That feeling of separation is the illusion that has allowed our culture to become so materialistic and self-centred.

An awareness of the family of humanity is the second dimension of awareness. This is what helps us to understand others, to value fairness and justice, and to be compassionate where previously we would have been prejudiced or indifferent.

This awareness also allows us to give our greatest gift to other people, our listening. When we truly listen to other people we understand their real depth and individuality. We see a far richer picture than the alternative, a snapshot of assumptions and guesses. But for the other person that listening is even more powerful still. When we are truly heard by someone who sees Possibility within us we are liberated, a healing has begun. That is the most valuable supreme offering we can give each other, it is the basis for building the one human family that together can create a Future Worth Choosing.

To me, it seems a terrible indignity to have a soul controlled by geography.
George Santayana

The earth is but one country and mankind its citizens.
Baha'u'llah

President Reagan pointed out to President Gorbachev in 1985 that a common threat to this planet from another would help the warring sides see their common humanity in an instant and begin to work together for the survival of us all. Today the threat is not from space but from the way we currently live with each other – can we still find our common humanity?
Our Planet Needs Us!

Seeing the big picture

The third dimension of Awareness is our relationship with Life itself, and for this Enquiry is the key. Now more than ever we need to be asking the big questions that take us to new and fresh thinking, to a higher level of Awareness. ☉

We can enquire through books, gurus or quantum physics, we can seek answers in a house of worship, a state of meditation or while walking the dog. It doesn't matter which we choose, because it is increasingly obvious that these different paths are converging. Quantum physicists now offer us the same notions as philosophers and spiritual leaders have been presenting throughout time.

So as Enquirers we have some fascinating possibilities to consider, one of the most important is that we are each linked to all other Life. Our thinking is changed forever just by considering this enormous idea.

Another possibility is that we can all reach into another level of knowing. This is not the product of our rational thinking, but a deeper wisdom that arises when we learn to tame our busy mind: **this is inspiration.**

Thus are we drawn into a different Awareness, in which we are likely to be curious and accepting rather than fixed and judgemental. As we deepen our Enquiry we begin to banish fear and anger to be more at peace with ourselves. We are more likely to be respectful and compassionate for the peoples and creatures of the earth.

For all these reasons Enquiry is the most powerful of the three dimensions of Awareness.

The deepest level of truth uncovered by science and by philosophy is the fundamental truth of the unity. At the deepest subnuclear level of our reality, you and I are literally one.
John Hagelin

The music of this opera was dictated to me by God; I was merely instrumental in putting it on paper and communicating it to the public.
Giacomo Puccini

My hand is entirely the instrument of a more distant sphere
Paul Klee

Ever **greater**

Awareness

Awareness is made up of these three different relationships, **with Self, Others and Life.** If we can develop our understanding of each of these simultaneously we will expand our Awareness.

A Future Worth Choosing requires higher Awareness. But equally this future is higher Awareness. We can see the elements of Fair Shares, Living Values, Respect for Gaia and Ever After Thinking as just the hallmarks of living at this Awareness. And Awareness sweeps out Ignorance and Denial, it helps us to resist Seduction and overcome Indifference and Impotence.

The five principles of Action simply become our natural behaviour: we want to live lightly, spend ethically, serve, shine and to speak out for this new life.

The treatment of Awareness in these pages is brief for a topic that warrants a lifetime of study and practice. So these ideas serve as a point of departure on a journey that can be trodden in a thousand different ways. The key is simply to be treading the path. This is what delivers a higher level of Awareness and makes possible the Action through which we make a visible difference in the world.

With Action and Awareness combined we have a journey of transformation for each of us individually and all of us together, a route to the Future Worth Choosing.

A new, spiritually based social activism is beginning to assert itself. It stems not from hating what is wrong and trying to fight it, but from loving what could be and making the commitment to bring it forth.
Elisabeth Kübler-Ross

answering the call

we started with a question:

can we save the human race from itself ?

The answer of course is a resounding Yes! We know that our Action and Awareness can fashion a Future Worth Choosing: we know we can build a sustainable way of life for humans here on Planet Earth.

This isn't a new idea, it isn't revolutionary, but it is an idea whose time has come. Its time has come now for three reasons, each of which have now become undeniable. Firstly, we now recognise we have gained the technology and the capability to be the co-creators of our human destiny. Secondly the converging crises of our age create an unprecedented and urgent need for action and change. Lastly we have identified an opportunity to respond to the world situation: we have found response-ability.

So the idea that we can build a Future Worth Choosing is an idea that cannot be resisted. We don't need to convince people of this because the idea can't be contested. It might make some feel uncomfortable, angry or guilty but the reality remains. Most important is that people decide where to stand in relation to this, as part of the solution or part of the problem.

Ron Monnier

individually
we make a difference

So let's go! Are you ready for the most important and exciting Work available here on the planet in the early years of the 21st century? Our task is to build a Future Worth Choosing. This requires our response motivated by a vision of future we can create, a mission of love rather that a fear-based reaction to our current plight. We will do this by accessing a higher level of collective Awareness than we have yet shown in humankind's history here. And we each have a vital role to play.

When any one of us stands for a Future Worth Choosing a ripple of light spreads around the world. So when you make this stand you begin to empower others to recognise their own inner calling, you are now a source of inspiration to others.

The moment you commit to be a Voice of the Future powerful, unseen forces are unleashed. As your Awareness grows, your relationships with yourself and others transform: you awaken to new understandings about the process of Life itself.

You become a dynamic force for change. Your Actions immediately start to have a transforming effect on the world around you. You make a difference with your energy, your money, even just a smile, and you become a role model for others who do as you do.

We each have a vital role to play individually. Remember: Your Planet Needs You.

The starting point for a better world is the belief that it is possible.
Norman Cousins

A lot of people are waiting for Martin Luther King or Mahatma Gandhi to come back -- but they are gone. We are it. It is up to us. It is up to you.
Marian Wright Edelman

together
we change the world

Let us join the growing mass of people around the world who want to answer the call, joyfully stepping into their own ability to respond to our world situation. These are people beginning to find within themselves a deep untapped sense of purpose, that unites their own unique skills and capabilities with the work required in building a Future Worth Choosing. And now we are beginning to connect and combine in whole new ways.

Then we form a critical mass, ready to cooperate and work together for the highest good of the human family. Our boundless creativity takes over, and there are ideas and projects aplenty to restore the planet to a state of well-being with which we can live in interdependence.

And we begin the work of recreating our structures of government, ensuring freedom and fairness are respected by those we trust to lead us. We redesign our economic models to make business a servant to humanity. We start to fashion the schools and universities which will teach future generations how to live in peace with each other.

Our crowning glory will be when we realise we are living entirely at peace and in balance with the natural world, a sustainable life for human beings: a Future Worth Choosing is ours!

We all have a vital role to play together.
Remember: Our Planet Needs Us.

It is better to light one small candle than to curse the darkness.
Confucius

The World needs an enormous number of new Innovators, Change Agents, and Transformers, all dedicated to turning Development in the direction of sustainability. People like you.
Alan Atkisson

In closing **we offer you this simple meditation**

Today I affirm again my stand for a Future Worth Choosing,
A just, peaceful and sustainable life for the entire human family and our natural world.
Help me to choose my thoughts and deeds to bring about to this future,
By living lightly, in balance with my planet home,
By directing my energy and money to make the biggest difference,
By serving those I love and the communities to which I belong,
By standing up and speaking my Truth,
By shining my light in the world for all to enjoy.

Help me to be the change I want to see in the world.

Give me the courage to be true to Myself and my Purpose.
Help me find a compassionate and loving relationship with the whole Human Family,
And help me continue to be open to new Awareness.
Help me to overcome fear and act in the world with Love,
Through this we will bring about the world we want,
And live a Future Worth Choosing Now !

P.S. it's a mission of Love

"Tell me the weight of a snowflake," a coal-mouse asked of a wild dove.

"Nothing more than nothing," was the answer.

"In that case I must tell you a marvellous story," the coal-mouse said. "I sat on a branch of a fir, when it began to snow. Since I didn't have anything better to do, I counted the snowflakes settling on my branch. Their number was exactly 3,741,952. When the 3,741,953rd dropped onto the branch, nothing more than nothing, as you say, the branch broke off."

Having said that, the coal-mouse flew away.

The dove, since Noah's time an authority on the matter, thought about the story for a while, and finally said to herself: "Perhaps only one person's voice lacking for peace to come to

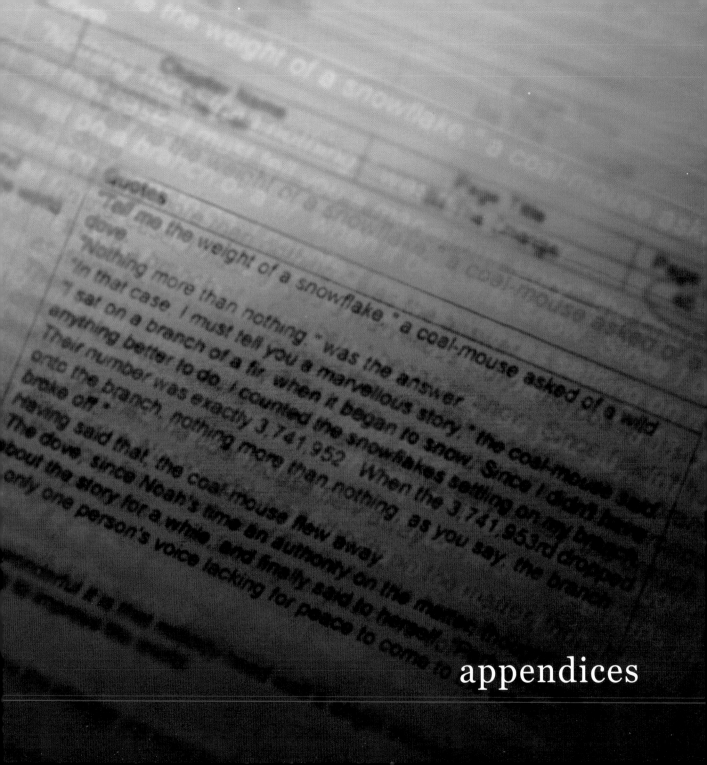

appendices

sources and resources

This section is intended to offer a summary of the both the sources used in compiling the book marked with the ☁ symbol and the resources readers can use to explore the ideas in more depth. We have tried to select websites relevant to an international audience wherever possible.

CHAPTER 1: A Future Worth Choosing

Page 9: The term 'Future Worth Choosing' is taken directly from Morel Fourman's excellent book, Personal and Global Transformation, (Morel Fourman, 2005). We heartily recommend his work as a very practical guide to finding and working with Purpose. The phrase is used by kind permission of the author.

Page 11: The Earth Charter is a wonderful statement of principles and values for a sustainable future. Too lengthy to quote in this book it is however well worth studying. Endorse it on their website, www.earthcharter.org.

Page 12: The WHO story is quoted on the Harvard University Graduate School of Education website, www.pz.harvard.edu.

Page 13: The Gaia Theory, that the earth is a living system, is from James Lovelock's book, Gaia: A New Look at Life on Earth, (Oxford University Press, 1979).

Page 15: This definition of sustainability is drawn from the report of the Brundtland Commission, Our Common Future, published in 1987 and sponsored by the United Nations. It is one of the most widely used definitions of this concept.

Page 16: The concept 'an idea whose time has come' is wonderfully articulated in Werner Erhard's essay 'The end of starvation: creating an idea whose time has come', written for The Hunger Project. We have a paper copy of this but can find no reference to where this work might be stored or how it can be obtained. The Hunger Project can be explored at their own website, www.thp.org.

CHAPTER 2: How We Shape the World

Page 19: Calculations are based on an article in Reclaiming Politics (IC#30), Fall/Winter 1991, Your Bicycle is Faster, and on the inspiring web site set up by the late Ken Kifer, www.kenkifer.com.

Page 20: The work of Dr Emoto can explored in his two books, The Message from Water, (Hay House, 2006), and The Hidden Messages in Water, (Pocket Books, 2005). And check out his websites, www.hado.net and www.masaru-emoto.net.

Page 25: TV statistics from Your Child; Development and Behavior Resources, Developmental and Behavioral Pediatrics at the University of Michigan.

Page 27: Marianne Williamson shares great insight into the influence of fear in our lives, most particularly in her best-known work, Return to Love, (Harper Collins, 1992).

We have heard the mnemonic FEAR from several sources, most recently in a public lecture by inspirational speaker Ali Atwell.

CHAPTER 3: A Snapshot of Our World

Page 32: Statistics are all from the Make Poverty History resources; a booklet of that name, (Geraldine Bedell, Penguin Group, 2005), and the website www.makepovertyhistory.org.

Susan George provides a clear and disturbing account of how the world trade system operates in her very readable book, Another world is possible if . . . (Verso, 2004).

Page 34: Statistics on the human lives lost to poverty related conditions can be obtained in several places and show some small variation. The number of 50 000 deaths per day is quoted by Make Poverty History.

The global ice cream market is estimated at $47 billion a year, according to Euromonitor data quoted by market leader Nestlé.

Page 36: Arms sales figures from annual report on the arms industry from the Stockholm International Peace Research Institute; world military expenditure in 2004 is estimated to have been $1.03 trillion in current dollars.

The cost of universal primary education is quoted from Make Poverty History data.

Page 38: The concept 'ancient sunlight' and the population estimate supported by 'current sunlight' are from the book, The Last Hours of Ancient Sunlight, by Thom Hartmann, (Hodder and Stoughton, 2001).

Estimates of the rate of destruction of the rain forest vary and there is no consensus about how much remains. The site at www.rainforestweb.org is an excellent portal through which to find out more about all aspects of the rain forest.

The state of world fisheries can be explored in detail on the website of the International Council for the Exploration of the Sea, which is www.ices.dk.

The figures on grain production and topsoil erosion were sourced from the Earth Policy Institute at www.earth-policy.org.

The statement about the number of people affected by water shortage is by UN Secretary-General Kofi Annan, in We The Peoples, 2000.

Ice shrinkage figures are as quoted on website of the American Natural Resources Defense Council, www.nrdc.org.

Page 40: The whole topic of climate change can be researched extensively online, where a full range of views are available. Amidst all of the information there are 3 sites that offer a good and relatively objective view; these are
www.defra.gov.uk/environment/climatechange/index
www.exploratorium.edu/climate
www.bbc.co.uk/climate

For a discussion of the consensus in the scientific community see Naomi Oreskes excellent essay published at
www.sciencemag.org/cgi/content/full/306/5702/1686

For information on the Sea Ice melt
http://news.independent.co.uk/environment/article351135.ece from 14 March 06 Independent Newspaper
For information on the Tundra
www.guardian.co.uk/climatechange/story/0,12374,1546824,00.html 11 August 05 Guardian
For information on the Oil industry lobby
www.guardian.co.uk/oil/story/0,11319,1502486,00.html
www.medialens.org/alerts/05/051206_burning_the_planet.php

The Elisabet Sahtouris quote is taken from a March 2006 press release issued by her office.

Page 44:   This is an edited excerpt from The Hundredth Monkey by Ken Keyes Jr. (Devorss & Co 2nd edition June 1984).

CHAPTER 5: What We Can Do

Page 50:   Live Lightly on the Planet
There is a fast-growing selection of books on this topic in every bookstore now. I like and recommend The Better World Handbook: Ellis Jones, Ross Haenfler, Brett Johnson, Brian Klocke, (New Society Publishers, 2001).
Reduce, Reuse, Recycle: Nicky Stott, (Green Books, 2004). Do the Right Things!: Pushpinder Khaneka, (New Internationalist Publications, 2004). A Good Life: Leo Hickman, (Eden Project Books, 2005).
There is also lots of information online, some of the easiest sites to use are
Recycling: www.obviously.com/recycle
www.epa.gov/epaoswer/non-hw/muncpl/reduce.htm
www.reducereuserecycle.co.uk
Reducing Energy Use:
www.eere.energy.gov/consumer
www.est.org.uk
Living Simply: www.simpleliving.net
www.enough.org.uk

The footprint data was obtained from the World Wildlife Fund's excellent Living Planet Report 2004

Page 54:   Make Your Money Make a Difference
Many of the books referred to in the previous section also cover this element of Action. In the UK the magazine Ethical Consumer (www.ethicalconsumer.org) offers detailed views about products and suppliers.

In addition there are several websites with good and thought provoking information.
www.fairtrade.org.uk
www.maketradefair.com
www.greenmoneyjournal.com
www.verdant.net
www.ethicalconsumer.org/boycotts/boycotts_list.htm
www.newtithing.org
www.justgive.org

Find out all about charity gifts, the smart answer to all of those "what shall I buy so-and-so?" quandaries.
www.charitygifts.com
www.greatgifts.org/GiftSelection/home.aspx

The Tesco sales data is from TNS market research data, freely available on the web. The Wal-Mart data from Wal-Mart and the American National Retail Federation.

Page 57:   More information about 'Penny' can be found at www.penny-on.org

Page 58:   Be of Service
www.vso.org.uk
www.volunteering.org.uk
www.volunteermatch.org
www.worldwidevolunteering.org.uk
The health benefits of volunteering are quoted in "The Healing Power of Doing Good", by Allan Luks.

Page 60:   Stand Up Speak Out
www.writetothem.com
www.citizen.org.uk
www.ethical-business.com
www.charter88.org.uk
www.amnesty.org.uk
The Member of Parliament quoted is Christine Russell, MP for Chester, in personal conversation with the author. The BBC view was also expressed in personal correspondence with the author.

CHAPTER 6: Awareness
Page 68:   Recommended further reading is Personal and Global Transformation, the Morel Fourman book already referenced above, and Authentic: How to Make a Living by Being Yourself by Neil Crofts.

Page 70:   This anecdote was revealed by both men; Reagan in a speech at the Fallston High School in Maryland on December 4, 1985; Gorbachev on February 17, 1987 in the Grand Kremlin Palace in Moscow to the Central Committee of the USSR's Communist Party.

Page 72:   The Quest is a framework for personal and spiritual development. It is published and available through The Quest Partnership which can be reached through their website, www.thequest.org.uk.

CHAPTER 7: Answering The Call
The principal resource recommended here is www.yourplanetneedsyou.org.

Other books not referred to directly in Sources and Resources are;

50 facts that should change the world: Jessica Williams, Icon Books 2004
Change the World for a Fiver: We Are What We Do, Short Books, 2004
Conscious Evolution: Barbara Marx Hubbard, New World Library, 1998
Critical Mass: Philip Ball, Arrow Books, 2004
How We Can Save the Planet: Mayer Hillman, Penguin, 2004
If the World Were a Village: David J. Smith, Shelagh Armstrong, A & C Black, 2003
Mid-Course Correction: Ray C. Anderson, Chelsea Green Publishing Company, 1998
No Logo: Naomi Klein, Flamingo, 2001
Our Final Century: Martin Rees, Arrow Books, 2003
Philip's Guide to the State of the World: Philip's, 2004
Power vs. Force: David R. Hawkins, Hay House, 2002
Spiritual Politics: Corinne McLaughlin and Gordon Davidson, Ballantine Books, 1994
The Awakening Earth: Peter Russell, Ark Paperbacks, 1982
The Corporation: Joel Bakan, Constable, 20004
The Ecology of Commerce: Paul Hawken, Weidenfeld & Nicolson, 1993
The Rebirth of Nature: Rupert Sheldrake, Rider 1990
The Rough Guide to a Better World: Martin Wroe and Malcolm Doney, Rough Guides, 2004
The Tipping Point: Malcolm Gladwell, Abacus, 2002
Vital Signs 2003-2004: Worldwatch Institute, Earthscan Publications, 2003

Illustrators and contributors

Listed below are the talented individuals who have
contributed their services and skills to this book, they all
contributed work free of charge because they believe in the
cause please support them by visiting their websites and
use their services.
Illustrator and agent nick diggory, www.nickdiggory.com

www.theillustrators.org
The Association of illustrators www.aoi.org
Thanks for the globe Angela
All other Illustrations and photographs have been created
by Phil Turner, www.philturner-uk.com

P7	Alisa Murray	www.alisamurray.com
P8	Ron Monnier	www.ronmonnier.au.com
P10	Ann Ellis	www.annellis.co.uk
P12,13	Lee Woodgate	www.leewoodgate.com
P14	Christian Skjott	www.fflys.com
P18	Ian Pollock	www.ianpollock.co.uk
P20,21	Photos by Dr Emoto	
P22	Maxwell Paternoster	www.maxwellp.co.uk
P28	Brent Hardy Smith	tel:01663 745 564
P39	Linzie Hunter	www.linziehunter.co.uk
P41	Phil Disley	www.phildisley.com

P43	Holly DeWolf	www.sweethappy.ca
P53	Photo by Jack Symes	
P57	Penn logo is © to GSR	penny-on.org
P61	Phil Disley	www.phildisley.com
P62	Happy heads by Sophie and Harry Turner	
P63	Ben O'Brien	www.bentheillustrator.com
P65	Pellenesa	
P71	Deborah Everton	www.deboraheverton.com
P77	Ron Monnier	www.ronmonnier.au.com
P78,80	Sophie Turner	

ypny

The Authors - two blokes on a mission

Jon

2003 was the turning point for me, the 'story' wasn't working for me anymore. In a world which seems so broke it was no longer an option to just continue to live as I did, to all appearances a happy, successful life in our western, material understanding of that concept. I gave up my ambitions to build a large consulting business, down-shifted and made the space for something new to emerge. This book is the product of all of the reflection and inspiration that followed and is just one of the ways in which I will continue to help in the amazing awakening which is sweeping around the world. So all of the experience I have gained as a speaker, coach, consultant and entrepreneur plus the lessons I am still learning as a father, lover and a friend will be channelled into the YPNY project and this wonderful work. One of my friends told me "You'll never change the world from Chester." I don't agree, we can all make the world a better place from wherever in it we are; this book is my best shot at doing so.

Phil

When Jon asked me to design this book I was delighted to accept the challenge. My creativity was stifling and needed a vehicle; the timing was perfect. In a world where manners, empathy, decency and compassion are brushed aside to get to the shops or secure the next deal, its time we changed. We are living in a period, a point of time on a graph, a part of the history of the human race on earth. We study other periods in our time on earth, art, philosophy, religion, technology, and war. So where does the 21st Century fit in?

Mass consumerism runs alongside war, it's feast or famine. Excess in everything, food, water, sex, alcohol, drugs, products, pleasure. Are we really designed to live like this? Some people survive eating man made chemicals shaped into food and other people make a living advertising it to them, day after day, year after year, deceptive marketing keeps us upgrading to newer versions. But "aren't we just trying to create a better life for our family, a loving, happy life - for ourselves, why shouldn't we?" Yes we should, but its how we do it and the way we teach our children that will shape the future.

REALISE THIS. The world has to change, and at some point it will. Be part of that change today.

My love and thanks to Jon Symes for presenting me with a wonderful gift and to Trish for helping me see it.

Your Planet Needs You

To explore this fast-growing movement visit them at www.yourplanetneedsyou.org

Contact the Authors

Jon Symes	e	jon@yourplanetneedsyou.org
	t	+44 (0) 1244 677194
	m	+44 (0) 7767 216520
Phil Turner	e	phil@yourplanetneedsyou.org
	t	+44 (0) 161 439 1669
	m	+44 (0) 7747 624590